Rubber Stamping

Dedication

In loving memory of 'Ammie' and 'Cyril Squirrel' whose legacy has been the knowledge that with good friends and family you can survive all things.

To my Mum for the gift of creativity.

To Jenni, Becki, Jason, Megan and Reece, my wonderful children and grandchildren, without whose support I would not have made it this far.

And to Anna my chauffeur, chaperone and helpmate. Thank you all.

Rubber Stamping

Kim Reygate

SEARCH PRESS

First published in Great Britain 2006

Search Press Limited
Wellwood, North Farm Road,
Tunbridge Wells, Kent TN2 3DR

Text copyright © Kim Reygate 2006

Photographs by Roddy Paine Studios

Photographs and design copyright © Search Press Ltd. 2006

Hardback: ISBN-10 1-84448-240-5
ISBN-13 978-1-84448-240-5

Paperback: ISBN-10 1-903975-86-7
ISBN-13 978-1-903975-86-2

The Publishers and author can accept no responsibility for any
consequences arising from the information, advice or instructions
given in this publication.

Suppliers
If you have difficulty in obtaining any of the materials and equipment
mentioned in this book, then please visit the Search Press website for
details of suppliers: www.searchpress.com

Publishers' note

All the step-by-step photographs in this book feature the author,
Kim Reygate, demonstrating rubber stamping. No models have
been used.

Manufactured by Universal Graphics Pte Ltd, Singapore

Printed in Malaysia by Times Offset (M) Sdn Bhd

Acknowledgements

I would like to extend my heartfelt thanks to all those
who have helped make this book a reality.

Special thanks to Hazel at Horseshoe Craft, Wendy
at Stamps and Memories, Julia at Simply Stamps,
Linda at LB Craft, Teresa and Faye at Creative
Pastimes and Judith at Woodware for all their help
with just some of the products used in the making of
this book.

I would like to thank the following companies for
kindly allowing me to use their superb stamps:
Hobby Art, Elzybells Art Stamps Ltd., Paper
Inspirations Inc., Impression Obsession, Magenta,
Friends Stamps, Heritage Rubber Stamp Co., Hero
Arts, Paper Parachute, Stamps Happen, Penny Black,
Stampendous, Judikins and Stamp-It.

My thanks also to George at Artwrap for use of the
Kandi Kane hot-fix tool and to Coppernob for the
M and F board.

I also want to thank the team at Search Press for their
help, to Katie my editor, and to Roddy for once
again exhibiting endless patience and supplies of
coffee during the photo shoot.

But in particular I would, once again, like to extend
my sincere thanks to Anna for always being there
when I needed her support or a well placed kick in
the pants when it came to writing the words. I could
make cards for England but when it comes to words
I'm no JK Rowling and so for Anna's assistance with
this I will be eternally grateful.

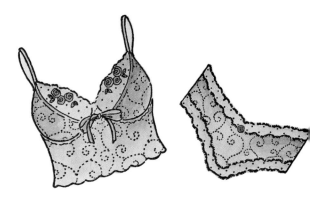

Contents

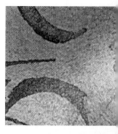

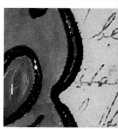

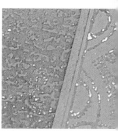

Introduction

My first encounter with rubber stamping came at a needlecraft show in 1996. I had always been a cross-stitcher but found myself fascinated by this new craft. I had never seen it demonstrated before but it seemed like fun and I felt that it could be used to enhance my cross-stitch cards. I attended some classes and after my first introduction I became a self-confessed 'stampaholic' – my journey to the writing of this book had begun.

My addiction did not stop at rubber stamping and I have gone on to try all manner of papercrafts, though my first love has always remained stamping. I now teach rubber stamping and paper crafting, and demonstrate for a variety of craft companies. More recently I have written articles for several craft magazines and a book on tea bag folding, which was published by Search Press in 2003. In 2005 I was lucky enough to be voted into third place for Card Designer of the Year, an honour for which I feel extremely proud.

It is a tremendously addictive journey upon which you will embark when you open this book. It is one that will fill you with hours of pleasure and enable you to delight your friends and family with your handmade creations. I have a friend who each year unwraps my Christmas cards along with the decorations and places them on the mantelpiece in happy anticipation of the next arrival to add to her collection!

I have never considered myself to be a particularly creative person – I thought that you had to be able to draw to be that. Rubber stamping has enabled me to prove otherwise, and I hope that this book will help you, too, to fulfil your own creative potential.

Kim x

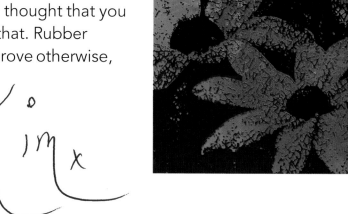

Materials and equipment

Stamping isn't scary, it's fun, but there are so many different products out there, with new ones coming on to the market at a seemingly daily rate, that to the novice it can all seem a very daunting prospect. All I can say is enjoy, and don't be afraid to experiment.

To create your first hand-stamped item, there are some basic pieces of equipment you will need. Your choice depends on many things: availability, personal preference and, of course, what you wish to make. You do not need to buy everything at once – add stamps and other supplies as you go along. To start with, it is better to invest in a few good quality tools which can be added to as you progress. As you become more experienced, you will find many uses for your ever-expanding collection of equipment.

Remember, there are very few rules, if any – just enjoy!

Rubber stamps

These are available from a wide range of companies and come in all shapes and sizes. They are no longer restricted to the traditional wood-mounted stamps – foam, clear and rubber unmounted stamps are now available, which often come as large, multiple-image sheets. There are also transparent polymer stamps, which can be removed from their clear blocks making them easy to position, and stamps that are attached to a block magnetically.

Each type has its own particular advantage, but at the end of the day your choice of stamp will almost certainly come down to image. Some people prefer a solid image while others choose a stamp with fine detail. Whatever your preference, there is a stamp available to suit every style and occasion.

Inks and inkpads

As the photograph indicates, inkpads come in an ever-expanding variety of shapes and sizes. Large, small, shaped, single-colour, multicoloured, fixed and removable pads are available. However, unlike stamps, certain inks and inkpads are more suitable for certain types of card or paper.

Regular paper and card is porous, coated paper is not, therefore a degree of experimentation is required to establish which inks work best for you on any given surface. Most, if not all, inkpads will have a certain amount of information provided with them on how they should be used. Read it, but never be afraid to try them out in different ways.

As a general rule, dye-based inks are quick drying, suitable for what is known as 'flat stamping'. Pigment inks are slower drying and are designed to be heat embossed. A dye-based inkpad generally has a more solid, felt-like base whereas a pigment inkpad is of a more spongy consistency to accommodate the thicker ink. Dye-based inks therefore lend themselves particularly to fine, detailed images since a too heavy application of the thicker pigment-type ink will almost certainly lead to a blurred or smudged image. If, like me, however, you love the look of heat embossing you will find that most dye-based inks will stay wet long enough to be coated with embossing powder, provided that it is applied immediately after stamping the image.

At the end of the day there should be no reason why you can't try any kind of ink on any surface. Experiment – the possibilities are endless. The following is by no means a definitive guide to all the types of ink available, but merely an indication of just a fraction of what is available in an ever-expanding market.

Dye-based ink

Water-based, quick-drying inks available in a wide range of single-colour and multicoloured pads.

Permanent ink

Suitable for use with glossy card and acetate. Care must be taken when stamping on these surfaces in order to avoid the stamp sliding. You will require a solvent-based stamp cleaner since a water-based cleaner alone will not remove permanent ink from the stamp.

Pigment ink

This is a slow-drying ink which makes it suitable for heat embossing. A quick-drying pigment ink is available which does not need to be heat set and works well on vellum, pearlescent and metallic card.

Watermark ink

This gives a wonderful watermark effect to any matte-finish card or paper. When used, it will create an image that is one or two shades darker than the colour on which it has been stamped. It takes a very long time to dry and is therefore probably best heat set.

Clear resist

This is an ink specially formulated to repel water-based dye inks; it must be heat set. An image stamped in clear resist will 'pop out' as if by magic when dye-based ink is applied over the top of it.

Chalk pads

These are pigment inkpads which dry with a matte chalk finish, as their name suggests.

Papers and card

You can make or break a good design by your choice of colour, texture and weight of paper or card. For greetings cards, a good quality, reasonably heavyweight card is best as a base. This can be a readymade card blank or a piece of card cut to size to suit your own project.

When layering, thinner decorative cards and papers can be used, such as vellum, mulberry paper, pearlescent papers, pre-printed patterned wrapping paper, serviettes, etc.

Adding colour

As can be seen from the photograph below, there is yet again a myriad of different ways in which colour can be added to a design, for example using embossing powders, chalks, watercolour paints and pencils, inks, pearlescent powders, mica-based paints and spritzing sprays, solid-block paint palettes, colouring pencils, felt-tip pens and brush markers. Glitters, glues and glazes can all be used to achieve beautiful results, and some stunning special effects.

As with papers and card, choosing the right colouring medium and application can make all the difference to your finished project.

Just some of the ways of adding colour to your designs.

Equipment

A few pieces of basic equipment are needed when you first start rubber stamping, but this can be expanded as your experience and knowledge develop. There will always be certain aspects of rubber stamping that you prefer over others, and this will automatically determine your choice of 'essential' equipment. If you are like me, you will end up trying everything and it will all find its way on to your 'must have' list of stamping essentials.

My suggested list of basics for the absolute beginner, which no doubt some of you will argue with, would include a cutting mat, a cutting implement, be it scissors, a craft knife or a guillotine, and some form of adhesive.

Listed below are all the pieces of equipment used in the book.

Adhesives

Everyone has their own favourite means of sticking their work together. Mine is double-sided sticky tape ('DSST'). Using it means that all layers remain firmly attached. Just some of the many other types of adhesive available are glue pens, heat-activated gluepads, repositionable spray adhesive, sticker machine, PVA glue, silicone sealant, 3D adhesive foam squares and adhesive dots.

Bone folder

This is a shaped tool that enables you to score and fold card to create a crisp, professional finish.

Cutting equipment

This again is very much a personal preference. A guillotine or paper trimmer is not essential to the rubber stamper's equipment list,

but you may find that it becomes a 'must have' as it speeds up your card cutting and can lead to greater accuracy.

Plain scissors or fancy-edged scissors can be used to cut paper or card, but a craft knife and metal ruler can be more accurate. A self-healing cutting mat is an essential piece of equipment when using a craft knife as it protects your work surface. For aligning and measuring more easily while you work, use a gridded cutting mat.

Old CD

This makes an excellent palette for use with both inkpads and marker pens.

Heat gun

There are several types of heat gun available and it is an essential piece of equipment if you intend to do heat embossing. A hairdryer is not suitable as it blows the powder around rather than heating it, although there is a type of heat tool that looks like one.

Cotton wool balls

These are my preferred way to apply chalks, but make-up applicators can also be used to great effect.

Dimensional glaze

Apply directly on to your artwork for a raised finish, or as a dimensional glue for glitter and beads.

Eraser

Essential for removing unwanted pencil or chalk marks from your work.

Hot-fix tool

A wonderful gadget for hot-fixing crystals, studs and pearls to both card and fabric.

Scoring, folding and box-making board

This is an amazing, but simple, piece of equipment which I find invaluable when it comes to scoring and folding my own greetings cards and making boxes (see page 20).

Punches

As with stamps and inkpads, these are available in all manner of shape and size. They are used to cut repeat images and shapes from thin card and paper.

Paintbrushes

These are used not only to paint with but also to apply pearlescent mica powders. I use fine brushes for detailed work and thick ones for removing excess powder, but the choice of brush is a personal one. A water-brush is great for watercolouring as it has its own reservoir and no pot of water is required. There is therefore no danger of spillage, and no need to continually redampen your brush. I also keep thin household bleach, which I use to bleach out colour, in a water-brush.

Positioning tools

These include a ruler, an eyelet positioner and a stamp aligner, all of which help in the creation of truly stunning designs.

Pencil sharpener

To sharpen your pencils and watercolour crayons.

Stamp cleaners

There are many methods of cleaning your stamps, including alcohol-free wipes. Damp kitchen paper is ideal for cleaning water-based inks from your stamps, and an old toothbrush will help to remove any stubborn patches of ink. Never run your foam-mounted stamps under a tap! If you have used a permanent ink then a special solvent-based stamp cleaner will be required.

Sponges and dabbers

Synthetic or natural, these are wonderful for applying texture and colour to your work.

Spaghetti (uncooked)

This has become an essential part of my crafting equipment since a friend taught me that it is a great way to pick up and apply non hot-fix crystals to your work – simply moisten the end.

Tweezers

Fantastic for holding and attaching tiny or intricate pieces to your work. Essential for applying craft stickers.

Embellishments

Almost anything can be used to embellish and enhance a design. Just some of the items used throughout this book include buttons, crystals, foil, wire, ribbon, punched shapes, craft stickers, embroidery and metallic threads, gold leaf and gold-leafing pens, paper fasteners and brads.

A well-placed ribbon, crystal or sticker can finish off a project. But do learn when to stop. Less is very definitely more when it comes to embellishments.

Basic techniques

There are two main types of stamp available – solid images and fine-detail stamps. Solid stamping, as its name suggests, produces a bold, solid image with little or no detail. A solid-image stamp works extremely well with pigment or embossable inks. Fine-line stamps contain far more detail than solid-image stamps and are used to create an image that can be coloured in. This is great if, like me, you cannot draw!

Whichever type of stamp you choose, I would advise using the same technique when inking it up. It is generally better to hold your stamp upside down (face up) and gently tap it all over with your inkpad, taking the pad to the stamp rather than the other way around. This way you have much more control over the amount of ink that you place on your stamp and are therefore less likely to over-ink it, which can lead to a blurred or smudged image. The exception to this rule is the dye-based multicoloured inkpad (see page 15).

Press firmly all over the back of the stamp once you have inked it and placed it on to your paper or card. This will ensure that all of your image is stamped out properly, and is particularly important when using large background stamps. Hold on to the item or piece of card you are stamping firmly as you lift your stamp, particularly when stamping on to glossy card, as the stamp has a tendency to stick to it.

Using a pearlescent pigment-based inkpad

A pearlescent pad, as used here, is just one of the many pigment-type pads available.

1. Gently tap the inkpad repeatedly on to the stamp until the whole of the stamp is evenly covered in ink.

2. Apply the stamp to the paper or card and press down firmly.

3. Carefully lift off the stamp.

Using a multicoloured dye-based inkpad

It is important not to mix up the bands of colour in a multicoloured inkpad by spreading the ink across from one to the other when applying your stamp. For this reason it is usually better to keep the pad on the table and tap the stamp on to it. You can use this type of pad with either a large or small stamp. Try not to move the stamp around the pad too much when inking, instead positioning it in the same place each time you re-ink and keeping the stamp parallel to the lines of colour.

You are less likely to over-ink a stamp using a dye-based inkpad due to the solid nature of the pad itself.

2. Check to ensure that the stamp is well inked.

1. Apply the stamp to the inkpad.

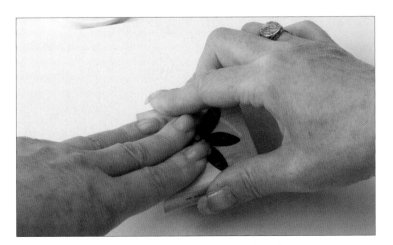

3. Transfer the stamp to the paper or card and press down firmly.

4. Carefully lift the stamp off the paper or card.

Colouring with a brush marker

This technique allows you much finer control over the placing of colour on the stamp. It is highly suitable when you wish to use a variety of different colours on a single stamp.

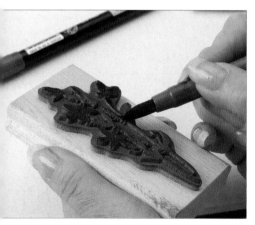

1. Apply colour gently to the stamp with the brush marker.

2. Before stamping, 'huff' on the stamp to remoisten the ink.

3. Apply the stamp to the paper or card, press down firmly and lift off the stamp.

Cleaning your stamp

Non-permanent ink can be wiped off your stamp with a damp cloth or alcohol-free wipe. Permanent ink needs to be removed using a solvent-based stamp cleaner. Always wipe over your stamp with a damp cloth or alcohol-free wipe after using this type of cleaner.

Applying solvent-based stamp cleaner.

Cleaning the stamp with an alcohol-free wipe.

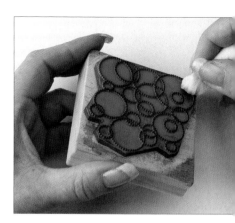

Cleaning the excess ink off a fine-detail stamp using an alcohol-free wipe. Paper towel or a cotton wool bud can also be used.

What can go wrong?

An under-inked stamp and image

Under-inking can be caused by a dry or worn-out inkpad. Applying the ink unevenly on to the surface of the stamp, or applying uneven pressure when stamping out the image, can both result in an under-inked look to the image.

An over-inked stamp and image

If you are too heavy handed when applying the ink to the stamp, ink can be transferred to the surrounding rubber, which can then result in a messy stamped image with unwanted portions of the rubber being stamped out as well as the image itself. Over-inking is more likely to occur when using a new inkpad, or when using pigment-type pads which have a much thicker ink.

A correctly inked stamp and image

With a little practice, it is easy to achieve a nicely stamped image on every occasion.

An over-inked fine-line stamp and image

Particular care needs to be taken when inking up a fine-line stamp since it is very easy to ink up the surrounding rubber as well as the image itself. For this reason it is usually best to use a dye-based ink, which is less thick than pigment-based ink. Although commonly perceived as a quick-drying ink used for flat stamping only, it is perfectly possible to heat emboss a dye-based ink so long as you are quick in applying the embossing powder to the stamped image. It will result in a beautiful stamped image losing none of the detail which can sometimes result from using a pigment-based inkpad.

The main elements in these two greetings cards were made from a sponged and flat-stamped piece of paper. This was created during the making of the project on page 20. Each panel created was then edged with a gold-leafing pen, and punched shapes and tiny, square craft stickers used to embellish the cards.

Sponging

Sponging is a wonderful way to achieve the most amazing multicoloured backgrounds. It is possible to add a wide diversity of colours and textures to your work by varying the type of sponge, the amount of pressure used or even whether the card is matte, glossy or textured. A previously stamped image can be sponged over, as in the purple panels in the three designs shown here, or a sponged background can be over-stamped to great effect.

Both pigment and dye-based inks can be used for this technique. Both will give their own specific 'look' to a project. My own particular favourite is the dye-based inkpad which I use to sponge over a previously stamped and embossed image. Areas of colour can be removed at this stage by applying thin, undiluted household bleach. This technique will only work when a dye-based inkpad has been used (see page 26).

All three of these designs were created from one sheet of hand-stamped and sponged background paper. The cross-hatched pattern was stamped several times in black dye-based ink and embossed in clear powder. This was then sponged over with purple dye-based ink. Various sized background panels were then cut from this.

The flower design was coloured using several small dye-based inkpads. Each stamped image came from the initial inking which, after stamping, was 'huffed' on (see page 16) to produce a paler subsequent image.

Purple Notes

For this project, you should begin by cutting eight sheets of plain white, good quality copy paper, though you can include as many pieces of paper as you wish. You could, of course, use ready-made notepaper instead.

I have made the notepaper 14 x 21cm (5½ x 8¼in) and used ready-made envelopes measuring 15 x 9cm (6 x 3½in), though you can make your own envelopes following the instructions on page 33.

To make the box I used a box-making board. The finished box lid measures 11 x 16cm (4¼ x 6¼in) and is 2cm (¾in) deep. The box itself is 2mm (¹/₁₀in) smaller than the lid all round, and is 2.5cm (1in) deep. Instructions for making the box are provided with the box-making board.

following the instructions on page 33.

You will need

- Rubber stamp (design 10277 by Magenta)
- Eight sheets of notepaper, either ready-made or pre-cut, 14 x 21cm (5½ x 8¼in)
- Eight ready-made envelopes, 15 x 9cm (6 x 3½in)
- Medium-weight, white card and box-making board
- Spare paper
- Self-healing cutting mat
- Rainbow dye-based inkpad
- Wedge-shaped make-up sponge
- Craft knife
- metal ruler
- 50cm (20in) narrow, purple ribbon

1. Work on a cutting mat with a spare sheet of paper laid over the top (this will help to protect your work). Take a sheet of the notepaper and mask off the part you do not want to ink using another piece of spare paper. Leave a 2.5cm (1in) border down the left-hand side. Have another piece of spare paper to hand.

2. To create the background to the design, begin by inking up the sponge. Dab it lightly on the green and purple section of the inkpad.

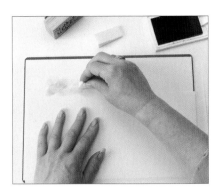

3. Apply the ink gently to the paper.

4. Dab the ink along the unmasked area of the paper. Turn the sponge slightly each time you apply the ink to avoid giving a uniform appearance to your design. Build up your own desired depth of colour. Allow the background to dry.

5. Now apply the pattern over the sponged background. Ink up the stamp, positioning it centrally over the purple and green section of the inkpad.

6. First stamp the image on to the spare piece of paper (this image could be used as the basis for the greetings cards shown on page 18) ...

7. ... then stamp the image on to the background. (Stamping it on to the spare paper first gives the image a softer appearance.)

8. Work your way along the length of the paper, creating a regular pattern over the background.

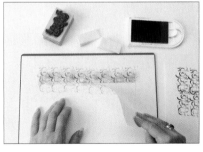

9. Carefully remove the mask, leaving a clean edge to your design.

The completed design.

10. For the detail, cut a paper mortise mask measuring 2 x 5cm (¾ x 2in). Leave a 0.5cm (¼in) border on the right of the mask, and a 1cm (½in) border at the bottom. Position the mask in the bottom right-hand corner of the paper.

11. Apply sponged ink over the mask following the same technique as before.

12. Stamp the pattern over the background as previously described.

13. Carefully remove the mask.

The box has been decorated all over with the same design as used on the notepaper.
The design was also stamped on to the envelopes. As an added touch, the sheets of notepaper were folded gently in half and bundled together with purple ribbon.

The notepaper and envelopes seen here are again made from good quality copy paper and ready-made envelopes. This time a torn mask has been used. On one set of paper and envelopes the sponged ink has been applied with a heavier hand. A notelet has been added to this set, and the sponged and stamped border enhanced by the addition of a mounted panel. Three metallic blue craft stickers have been added as a final embellishment.

To create the left-hand card, sponged background panels were cut to size and mounted on to darker card, having first been edged using a silver-leafing pen. The sizes of the borders were varied to add interest to the card. The stamped images were added last. The entire card was created using only one colour of inkpad.

The stamp used for the design of the middle card was coloured using brush markers. A masked panel was created on the left-hand side of a pre-folded card and the allium stamped repeatedly using the 'huffing' method described on page 16. It is amazing how many times an image will stamp out in this way, each slightly paler than the one before. This gives a soft feel to the card. The mounted panel was created in the same way. A fine-line silver craft sticker completed the look.

The flowered panel on the right-hand card was produced in the same way as the middle card, using brush markers. It was attached to a ready-made card that had been randomly masked and sponged with pearlescent ink.

These three cards use a similar stamped and embossed image as their main focus.
Each has been torn around the edge and mounted on to black glossy and gold card.

The top left-hand card and the bottom card each had a panel of stamped and
mounted branches added to them. The branches were stamped and embossed on to
card and were then painted with thin, undiluted household bleach. This will remove
some, if not all, of the colour from the card. (Bleach will not react with all card, so if
you intend to use this technique, experiment first.) The base card in each case was
sprayed with a mica-based spritz.

The top right-hand card was stamped and embossed with the branch image, then
thin, undiluted bleach was applied. A torn panel of vellum was attached using a spray
adhesive before the mounted panel with the embossed image on it was added.

Heat embossing

I have always considered heat embossing to be the 'wow' factor in any project. It is one of my favourite techniques and adds a truly elegant feel to a card for very little extra effort.

A slow-drying embossing ink is used to stamp out an image to which embossing powder is then applied. Embossing powders come in a wide-ranging variety of colours but in general an image is stamped using a clear embossing ink which then has coloured powder applied to it, or a coloured image is used with clear embossing powder applied.

This design was fashioned using gold, silver and copper embossed tiles. The original image was stamped out three times using a different colour of embossing powder each time. Every tile was then cut out and arranged in a pleasing design before being mounted on to black glossy card. Gold pearlescent card completed the metallic theme.

Evening Flower

Part of the fun of creating greetings cards is never quite knowing what size the finished card will be. For this reason I often use an A4 sheet of card as the basis for my design, as I can fold it in half and trim it to whatever finished size my project demands. This will often result in a card that is not of a standard size and will therefore require a handmade envelope. With this in mind, I have described an easy way to make an envelope that a friend shared with me (see page 33).

In this project, the size of your card may vary slightly from mine, depending on how you tear the paper panels.

When creating a layered design such as this one, always start with the top layer, in this case the stamped flower image, and work backwards, layer by layer, to the bottom. Embellishments can then be added to the finished design.

1. Work on a cutting mat with a sheet of spare paper laid over the top. Gently tap the clear embossing pad over the stamp, making sure the entire image is covered.

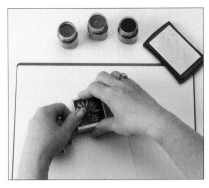

2. Apply the stamp to the piece of white card. Press down firmly then lift off the stamp, taking care to hold on to the card. You will be left with a sticky stamped image.

3. Gently shake the purple embossing powder in small patches over the stamped area, being careful not to cover it all.

4. Tap off the excess on to a spare sheet of paper folded in half and tip it back into the pot.

5. Cover some more of the remaining uncovered image with the dusky rose embossing powder.

6. Tap off the excess and return it to the pot as before.

7. Now cover the entire design in gold embossing powder to fill in any remaining gaps, and tip the excess back into the pot.

Tip

Leave the stamens free of rose and purple embossing powder so that they will be gold in the finished design.

8. Gently heat the image with the heat gun. As the powder reacts to the heat you will see it change to become raised and shiny. Do not overheat it. (Overheating can burn the card, and result in a flat, dull image.)

9. Tear around the image, leaving a border of approximately 0.5cm (¼in).

10. Colour the edges of the border by 'swiping' them gently with a red inkpad.

11. Apply thin strips of double-sided sticky tape to the back of the image. Partly peel back the top layer of each strip and fold to form a tab. This will allow you to position the image more easily.

12. Position the image on a piece of gold card. When it is positioned correctly, firm down the panel where the sticky tape is exposed and gently pull away the tabs to expose the rest of the tape and secure the image.

Tip

You may find it easier to use a craft knife to peel back the top layer of the double-sided sticky tape.

13. Trim off the gold card along the left- and right-hand sides and the top of the design, preferably using a guillotine, leaving a narrow gold border.

Tip

If you do not have a guillotine, use scissors or a craft knife and metal-edged ruler to trim off the card.

14. Tear the gold paper diagonally, starting approximately 1cm (½in) below the left-hand corner of the image. Tear the card towards you to expose a white layer along the tear.

15. Apply double-sided sticky tape to the back of the gold card, partly peel back the backing layer as before, and attach it to the sheet of glossy black card.

16. Trim the two sides and the top of the black card neatly, preferably using a guillotine, leaving a narrow black border. Tear the black card diagonally, just below the torn gold edge, as described in step 14.

17. Attach the design to the aubergine matte card using the same technique as before.

18. Trim the aubergine card, leaving a 1cm (½in) border (approximately) all round. Score and fold the red card, and trim it to be approximately 1cm (½in) larger than the aubergine card along the top and sides, and 1.5cm (¾in) deeper along the bottom.

19. Punch the corners of the aubergine card using the south-west corner punch.

20. Apply strips of double-sided sticky tape to the back of the aubergine card as before.

22. To embellish your card, use three black and three gold square craft stickers. Remove them from the sheet of craft stickers using a craft knife.

21. Attach the design to a sheet of white paper, and trim the edges to leave a narrow white border of approximately 1mm (¹/₂₀in). Finally, attach the design to the front of the card blank using double-sided sticky tape.

23. Position the three black craft stickers on the front of the card.

24. Position the three gold craft stickers, as illustrated.

Making an envelope

1. Place the greetings card on an A4 sheet of white paper. Fold up the paper from the bottom, so that just over half the card is covered. Push the card down to the fold.

2. Fold the top of the paper over to conceal the card, allowing a little room around it.

3. Turn the envelope over and sharpen the creases by running your fingers along them firmly.

4. Turn the envelope over again, and fold the top flap back, leaving approximately 3cm (1¼in) overlapping the bottom flap. This excess paper will be removed later.

5. Fold in the sides along the edges of the greetings card. Again, allow a little room all around the card.

6. Unfold the envelope and remove the card.

7. Score the folds using a bone folder.

8. Cut off the excess paper from the top flap with a guillotine. Trim the top and bottom flaps to the centre fold at a slight angle to the crease. Do the same with the side flaps.

9. Round off all the corners using a pair of scissors.

10. Fold in the sides of the middle panel and attach a strip of double-sided sticky tape to each side of the bottom flap. Form tabs (see card instructions, step 11), fold the bottom flap up and gently pull the tabs on the sticky tape to secure it.

11. Attach a strip of double-sided sticky tape to the inside edge of the top flap so that you can seal the envelope later.

12. Embellish the envelope to coordinate with the card. Use the leftover pieces of gold and black glossy card, and the gold square craft stickers.

The completed project, with a coordinating envelope.

Each of these cards uses the same stamped image as the project, but in very different ways. The first card (top left) was made following the same design but with a different combination of colours, altering the whole appearance of the finished card.

The gatefold card (top right) was created from bronze metallic card. The coloured panel on which the image is mounted was made using triangular pigment inkpads dragged gently but directly on to a piece of white card. This method is sometimes known as the direct to paper technique (DPT). The finished card is embellished with craft stickers and coloured metal studs.

The embossed panel of the bottom card has been closely trimmed to the image and simply mounted on to gold and black glossy card. A torn panel of metallic fibres has been added to the left-hand side with dramatic effect.

A multicoloured dye-based inkpad was used to create the background for this design. The floral panel was made using the same method as the main stamped panel on the cards shown opposite. It was then closely trimmed and mounted over a piece of lilac ribbon. Small, square, black craft stickers form the final embellishment.

The masked panel on the left-hand side of this design had flower and leaf craft stickers attached to it in a random pattern before the sponged colour was applied. The craft stickers were then removed and a crystal added to each flower centre. The floral panel was made in the same way as the main design on the cards opposite.

The three cards shown on the opposite page were all made using the same method, and indeed mostly the same stamps, however they each have a totally different feel. Each has a torn masked-and-sponged panel on the left-hand side. On this occasion I first randomly stamped and heat embossed a design using clear ink and white embossing powder. Colour was then sponged over the design. Even though I used a dye-based, quick-drying ink, it remained wet for a lot longer than normal because it had been worked into the card with the sponge. This meant that it was possible to sprinkle clear embossing powder over the entire image and heat emboss it. This can sometimes lead to a patchy finish, but I feel this adds to the handmade look of the finished card.

The stamped and mounted panel was created in the same way, this time using black dye-based ink and clear embossing powder for the initial stamped image. After the colour had been sponged over the image, thin, undiluted household bleach was painted over the flower petals. This removed some, if not all, of the colour. (This bleached effect can only be achieved using a dye-based ink.) The finished card was embellished with small shapes punched from another stamped and sponged image.

These three cards show how one stamp can be used in a variety of ways.
Additional mounting, craft stickers and vellum create three very different looks.

Sticky embossing

Sticky embossing can be used to add shine and sparkle to any stamped image, however detailed. It involves using an embossing powder which, once heated, remains sticky or 'tacky', and can therefore be used as an adhesive base for materials such as mica powders, chalks, foil and gold leafing – materials that would otherwise, and in my case less successfully, have to be attached using glue. Always remember, however, that sticky embossing powder should never be overheated or its stickiness will disappear.

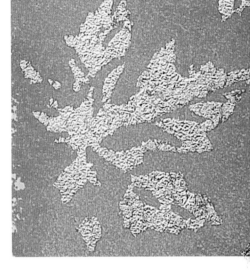

In this design, the central panel was created in a similar manner to the card below, but the shadow-stamped image was created by 'huffing' on the already-inked stamp from the previous design – two images for the price of one!

The central panel in this design was made using a shadow stamp inked with olive green, dye-based ink. The leaves were created using a second image stamped over the top using watermark ink and sticky embossing powder. This technique is described in detail in the following project.

Winter Sunshine

This project combines various types of card, paper and embossing powder to create something with a hint of glitz. I am not usually a lover of anything too sparkly – I leave the glitter glue to my granddaughter! However, I love the elegance of this card, achieved using sticky embossing powder, mica powders and foil.

In this project, you will make each layer of the card separately, starting with the square-shaped floral motif, before putting the various elements together to create the finished item

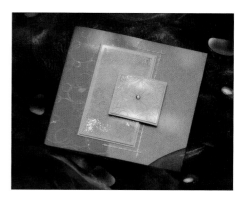

You will need

- Rubber stamps (Art Brush Vertical Palette G10194 by Paper Inspirations; Bubble Background by Friends Stamps; and design 32060F by Magenta)
- A5 sheet of white textured card
- Sheet of gold pearlescent card
- Lime green, pearlescent card blank, 13 x 13cm (5 x 5in)
- Sparkle vellum
- Spare paper
- Self-healing cutting mat
- Clear embossing pad
- Sticky embossing powder
- Teaspoon
- Heat gun
- Pearlescent pigment powders in lemon yellow, orange and light green
- Large and small paintbrushes
- Gold foil
- Double-sided sticky tape
- Repositionable spray adhesive
- 3D adhesive foam squares
- Guillotine or scissors
- Gold border craft stickers
- Gold-coloured hot-fix crystal
- Hot-fix tool
- Craft knife
- Tweezers

1. Work on a cutting mat with a sheet of spare paper laid over the top. First create the floral motif by applying embossing ink to the stamp and pressing it firmly on to the non-textured side of the white textured card.

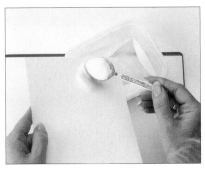

2. Cover the image with sticky embossing powder using a teaspoon.

3. Tap off the excess.

4. Heat the image with a heat gun. The white powder melts, leaving a clear, sticky image on the card. This only takes a few seconds. Do not overheat.

5. Apply lemon yellow pearlescent pigment powder randomly to the stamped image using a small paintbrush.

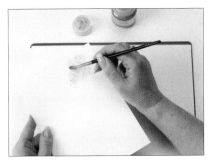

6. Fill in the gaps using orange pigment powder.

7. Tap off the excess powder on to a sheet of scrap paper.

8. Brush away any remaining powder on the image using a large paintbrush.

9. Press gold foil over parts of the design. Do not press too heavily as you do not want to over-foil the image.

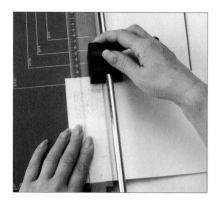

10. Trim off the card around the design, leaving a narrow border.

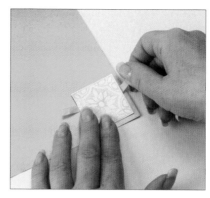

11. Apply thin strips of double-sided sticky tape to the back of the image. Partly peel back the top layer on each strip and fold it back to form a tab. Position the image on the gold card, then firm it down and gently pull away the tabs to secure it.

12. Cut out the design, leaving a gold border approximately 1mm ($^1/_{20}$in) wide. Take the sheet of white textured card, and apply clear embossing ink to the background stamp.

13. Stamp the background on to the textured side of the white card.

14. Sprinkle sticky embossing powder over the image, making sure it is all covered, and shake off the excess.

15. Heat the embossed image for a few seconds, until the embossing powder has melted. Do not overheat.

16. Use the large paintbrush to apply light green pigment powder over the whole of the background image.

17. Brush away any excess powder using the paintbrush.

18. Trim around the edges of the green background panel and apply patches of gold foil, as described in step 9.

19. Use double-sided sticky tape to attach the background image to the sheet of gold card.

20. Take the sheet of sparkly vellum and apply clear embossing ink to the circle-patterned stamp.

21. Stamp the image several times on to the vellum to create a patterned area approximately 8cm (3in) wide and 15cm (6in) deep.

22. Pour on the sticky embossing powder, shake off the excess and apply heat as before.

23. Use the large paintbrush to apply yellow, orange and green pigment powder to the image. Brush it on in patches using circular movements. When all of the pattern has been covered, tap off the excess on to a sheet of scrap paper and brush off any remaining on the vellum using the paintbrush. (Because the pigment colours have been mixed, do not return the excess powder to the pots.)

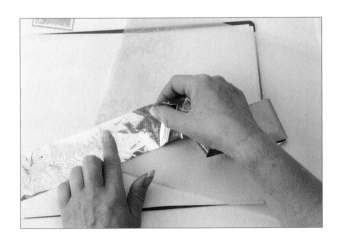

24. Apply patches of gold foil as before.

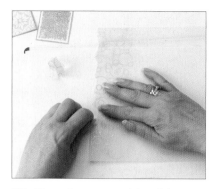

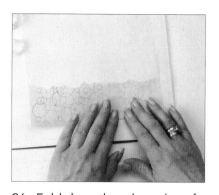

25. Tear down one side of the pattern to produce a torn edge.

26. Fold along the other edge of the coloured vellum leaving the foiled image uppermost. Trim off the excess plain vellum using either scissors or a guillotine, leaving a margin of approximately 3cm (1in) on the other side of the fold. This folded strip is used to attach the panel to the card.

27. Spray the back of the vellum with repositionable adhesive and attach it to the green card blank so that the pattern is on the front of the card.

28. Press the vellum down firmly on both sides of the card.

29. Open up the card and trim off the excess vellum.

30. Attach the green stamped background using double-sided sticky tape.

31. Place 3D foam squares on the back of the floral motif and remove the backing using a craft knife.

32. Position the motif on the front of the card using a pair of angled tweezers.

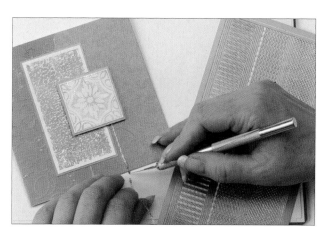

Make a coordinating envelope to add a finishing touch to a handmade greetings card (see page 33).

33. Attach gold border craft stickers to the two right-hand corners of the green background image. Trim off the ends with a craft knife.

34. Finally, attach a gold-coloured hot-fix crystal to the centre of the floral motif using a hot-fix tool.

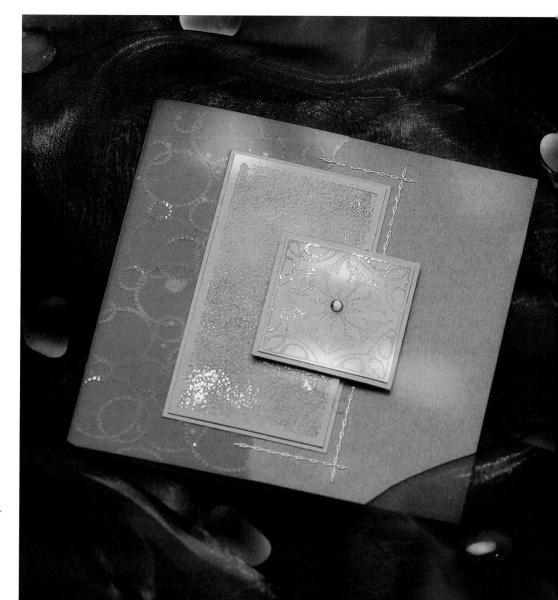

The completed project.

Sticky embossing, mica powders and foil were once again used to create the main element in the top left-hand card. Incorporating black glossy card into the mounting adds a very stylish feel.

Traditional gold, silver and bronze mica powders were used on the modern, geometric card shown top right.

Black glossy card has this time taken centre stage, in the unusual triangular card shown bottom right. Holographic foil was used, and the finished design embellished by the addition of fine-line silver craft stickers.

The design shown bottom left was created using a heat-activated gluepad. The leaves were stamped on to black glossy card using the gluepad. This image was then heated briefly until tacky and gold leaf applied. The excess gold leafing was removed with a stiff brush. The addition of a simply stamped tree completed this card.

The central floral vase on each of these three cards was created using a stamped and embossed image which was then coloured using a mica-based paint palette. Each card was then embellished using sticky embossing and foiling, following the same technique as used in the project. In the top two cards the foiling was applied to a panel which was then mounted on to the card. In the bottom card the sticky embossing and foiling was applied directly to the card.

The floral panel on the card shown at the top was coloured using traditional watercolour pencils. The stamped and sponged border completes this simple card.

When making a card, it is not always necessary to use the entire stamped image. The two middle cards use one section of a stamped image which was coloured using mica paints. The background around the flower was removed using a craft knife and the image mounted on to a backing panel. Torn vellum, complementary eyelets and craft stickers complete the designs.

The background to the bottom card was created by stamping and embossing a large design on to white card using clear embossing ink and white powder. A colour wash was then added. The background colour was mirrored in the main

Using colour

I am often asked 'What would be a good colour inkpad to buy?'. My reply is always the same: colour choice is a very personal one; my idea of a good colour may not be the same as yours. I love black and autumnal colours. I have never been a particular lover of orange, until I worked on the cards for this book. Sometimes we need somebody to suggest a colour to work with in order to avoid using our favourite colours over and over again. Whatever your choice, colour is available in a variety of mediums, resulting in a wide range of textures and styles.

Different colour combinations produce different effects. For example, use the three primary colours (red, blue and yellow), as in the card shown at the top on page 48, if you want to create a bright and cheerful design. For a more dramatic effect, use complementary pairs of colours (red and green, yellow and purple and blue and orange). For a more subtle look, put similar colours together, for example blues and purples or yellows and oranges. All colours can be made more or less intense by adding white, either in the form of white ink or paint, or by allowing more of the white background to show through. The bottom card on page 48, in which the colour of the flower is reflected in the paler background, is a good example of this effect.

These three designs each use an inkpad as the main source of colour. The chosen pad was tapped on to an old CD (see page 73) which was then used as a watercolour palette to paint the images. In the top two designs, the colour theme was continued in the stamped and sponged background. In the bottom design, the colours were mirrored in the backing card and decorative paper panel.

Autumn Spotlight

Spotlighting is a way of focusing on a particular portion, or portions, of a stamped design. Some stamped images, although incredibly beautiful, can appear daunting. By spotlighting – adding colour to only a small part of the image – the design becomes more achievable. It has enabled me to make use of stamps that might otherwise have remained unused due to the huge amount of colouring involved.

This project uses a randomly created background of colour which is then stamped over. A little bit of forward planning is required, since the inked background needs to dry before it can be used.

You will need

- Rubber stamp (Leaves Collage 90395 by Stamps Happen)
- Two sheets of white glossy card, each measuring 10 x 8cm (4 x 3¼in)
- Sheet of cream textured card, 28 x 14.5cm (11 x 5¾in), folded to make a card blank 14 x 14.5cm (5½ x 5¾in)
- A4 sheets of cream, non-textured card, black glossy card
- A4 sheet of matte card in turquoise and/or dark red
- Spare paper
- Self-healing cutting mat
- Dye-based ink in dark green, yellow, red and orange
- Black dye-based inkpad
- Clear embossing powder
- Heat gun
- Tweezers
- Fine-mist spray bottle filled with water
- Guillotine and/or scissors
- Small square punch
- PVA glue in a fine-tipped applicator bottle
- Double-sided sticky tape

1. Work on a cutting mat with several sheets of spare paper laid over the top (this stops the ink soaking through on to the cutting mat). Take the two sheets of white glossy card, and drip the ink on to one of the sheets in a random pattern. Apply four or five drops of each colour.

2. Spritz the card with water to spread out the drops of ink – be careful not to over-soak the card.

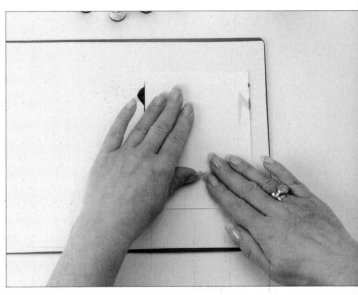

3. Lay the second sheet of card carefully over the first and firmly smooth the two layers together.

Tip

There are no hard-and-fast rules as to how many colours you can use in a multicoloured background like this, but a good rule-of-thumb is to use no more than four since any more than this can create a muddy finish.

4. Peel the two sheets of card apart, revealing the ink pattern.

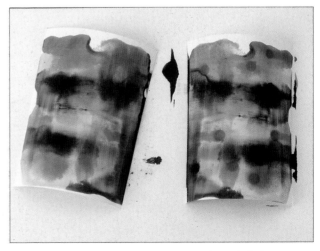

5. Leave the sheets to dry. They are best left for a couple of hours at least, preferably over night.

6. Once the background has dried, ink up the stamp using the black dye-based inkpad.

Tip

Dye-based ink is very good for detailed designs as it gives a clean, crisp image.

7. Stamp the image on to the non-textured cream card. Press firmly all over the stamp before lifting it off to ensure the entire image is complete. Pay particular attention to the corners.

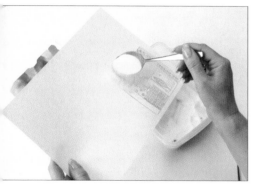

8. Quickly spoon on the clear embossing powder.

9. Tap the excess powder back into the container.

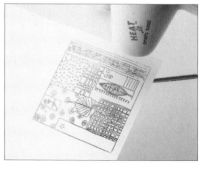

10. Heat the image using the heat gun.

11. Stamp the image on to the inked background.

Tip

Be very careful when applying the stamp to the inked background as it may slip on the glossy surface.

12. Apply embossing powder as before.

13. Heat the image using the heat gun.

14. Select the parts of the image you wish to highlight, and cut these out of the image stamped on the inked background. Cut just outside the black outlines.

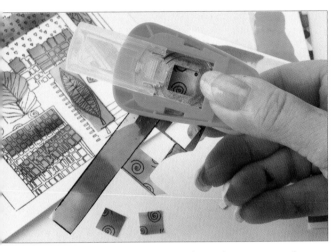

15. Retain the trimmings, and use them to punch out the three squares used to embellish the base of the card.

Tip

As you cut out the shapes you need, it is a good idea to place them in their equivalent positions on the image stamped on to plain card. This prevents them from getting lost, and gives you an idea of what the finished design will look like.

Tip

Use a very fine applicator for applying PVA glue to the smallest shapes.

16. Attach the coloured shapes to the image on the plain card. Use tweezers to place the shapes in the correct positions, and fix them in place using either PVA glue or, for the larger shapes, double-sided sticky tape.

17. Trim around the sides of the image and apply thin strips of double-sided sticky tape to the back. Partly peel back the top layer of each strip and position the image on the piece of black glossy card. When it is positioned correctly, remove the top layers of the strips of tape completely and press the image firmly in place. It is less wasteful to trim around the mounted image with scissors before neatening with a guillotine (if you have one) to create a 1mm (¹/₂₀in) black border.

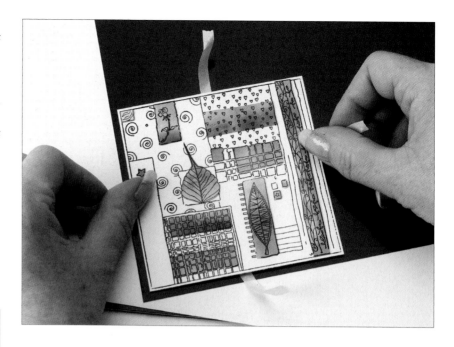

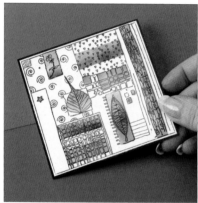

18. Hold the image against different coloured backgrounds before deciding which one to use.

19. Attach the image to your chosen background using double-sided sticky tape and trim it to size using either a guillotine or a pair of scissors. Leave a 0.5cm (¼in) border around the top and sides, and 2.5cm (1in) at the bottom. Mount the panel on to black glossy card and once again trim to leave a narrow border.

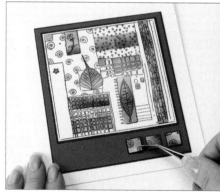

20. Attach the completed panel to the cream card blank and embellish it with the three punched squares you made earlier (step 15).

Tip

Personalise your card with the addition of a signature and a small, stamped image.

The completed project.

Although the card shown right was made in exactly the same way as the one above, it worked better with a dark red base card rather than the turquoise.

The left-hand card above was created in the same way as the one made in the project. A slight difference was the use of an oval punch. Thin, undiluted household bleach was painted on to the flower heads. (This bleaching technique will only work on dye-based inks.)
The right-hand card illustrates that it is not always necessary to use a complicated design when spotlighting.

The background on to which the peacock was stamped in the left-hand card (opposite) was created using a single-coloured, dye-based inkpad and several different shadow stamps. The card was further embellished using torn strips of a matching paper.
The background in the middle card was created in the same way, though using a multicoloured dye-based inkpad. The purple base card accentuates the purple in the peacock panel. Mulberry paper and craft stickers were used to further embellish this project.
For the right-hand card, mica paints were used to colourwash the white textured card and to colour the stamped and embossed image.

In the top card shown on page 58, a stamped panel was created using a clear watermark inkpad and single flower stamp. Chalks were then applied and further floral images produced and cut out individually. These were mounted on to the panel using 3D foam squares. Hot-fix crystals were used to complete the card.

This bottom right-hand card was created from a section left over from the chalked panel made in the previous card. Stamped and chalked vellum was added to the left-hand side of the card, and further embellishments added in the form of several punched tags and ribbon.

Chalked vellum was attached to the left-hand side of the final card. Three stamped and chalked images form the main elements of this design.

Using chalks

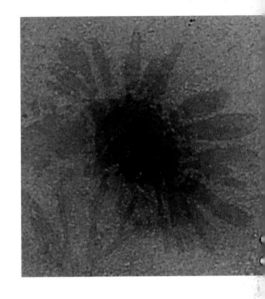

Chalk is a wonderfully easy means of adding colour to a card. My favourite way of applying the chalk, which I've used in the cards in this section, is using a cotton wool ball over a relatively solid stamped image. You can colour more detailed images by using the applicator supplied with your chalks, or a cotton wool bud. This produces a beautifully subtle image, but can be a difficult technique to master.

Torn coordinating card and gold craft stickers complement this pretty floral design.

A floral chalked panel layered on to black glossy card forms the centre piece of this design. It is mounted over a diamond pattern stamped and chalked directly on to the card.

Summer Daisies

This chalked card reminds me of hazy summer days. I like its soft, gentle look, which I achieved by using cotton wool balls to apply the chalk rather than applicator brushes. Whilst it may look complicated, it is actually quite easy to achieve. It just takes a certain degree of concentration and a few, well-placed masks.

1. Working on a gridded craft mat with a sheet of spare paper laid over the top, apply a background coating of yellow decorative chalk to the square cream card using a cotton wool ball. Apply the colour using small, circular movements.

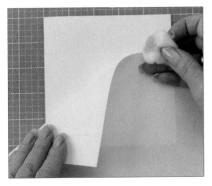

2. Remove the sheet of spare paper. Align the left-hand corner of the card with the grid marks on the mat. Place a sheet of scrap paper over the card, 4cm (1½in) from the top. Apply orange chalk over the exposed part of the card using the same technique as in step 1.

3. Turn the card round, align it with the grid as before and create a second overlapping orange strip.

4. Repeat on the remaining two sides.

Tip

Chalk can be rubbed out using a putty rubber if necessary.

5. Realign the card with the grid. Mask off the bottom and right-hand side leaving a 4cm (1½in) square exposed in the top left-hand corner.

6. Apply orange-red chalk to the card using the same technique as before. Leave the masks in place.

7. Ink up the flower stamp using the watermark inkpad. Align the flower head over the exposed orange corner and press down firmly.

8. Colour the flower by first applying yellow chalk, focusing on the central part of the flower, then adding orange to the remaining outer parts and finishing with a hint of orange-red applied to the tips of the petals and the lower part of the stem.

9. Repeat the flower design in the remaining three corners of the card.

10. Mask off the lower third of the card and stamp the first of the two images in the central square using the watermark inkpad.

11. Colour the flower in the same way as the four corner images

12. Re-ink the flower and stamp a second image in to the central square.

13. Colour the second image and remove the mask.

14. Stamp the small background image in the top right-hand corner of the centre of the card using the watermark inkpad.

15. Colour the stamped image using orange chalk applied with a cotton wool ball.

16. Stamp the small abstract design over the background.

17. Colour the design with orange-red chalk.

18. Spray the card lightly with hairspray (or chalk fixative) to fix the chalk.

19. Add the three gold, circular craft stickers as a final embellishment.

Complete the project by making a coordinating envelope (see page 33).

Making an insert

A truly professional finishing touch to any greetings card is the addition of a paper insert.

1. Cut a sheet of paper and fold it so that it is slightly smaller than the card. Attach a small piece of double-sided sticky tape on each side of the sheet, next to the fold.

2. Peel off the top layer of the tape and secure the paper inside the card.

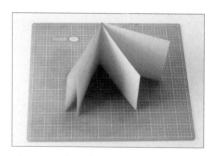

The completed insert.

The completed project.

These three cards are based on the same design as the project. Craft stickers and chalked vellum complement the unusually shaped floral panel on the right-hand card. The floral panel at the centre of the middle card was mounted on to complementary card stock which was then highlighted with chalks. This card was finished with a stamped and chalked border and hot-fix crystals. The top left-hand card was constructed using layers of complementary card stock, vellum and craft stickers.

Chalked panels were created in the top right-hand card using browns and greens mounted on to copper-coloured card. The main element was further embellished using a south-west corner punch and small punched flowers.

In the bottom card, the central chalked flower was layered on to a stamped and chalked background. Torn pre-printed vellum, matte-finished brads and punched squares completed this card.

The text on the top left-hand card was stamped directly on to a pre-scored white card before chalk was applied. Screwed-up paper forms the basis of the panel on the left. The flower was torn around before being attached to the card using 3D adhesive foam squares.

The top card in the picture has a strong, masculine feel to it. I have used a combination of stamped and mounted panels, a button and threads.

The two bottom cards both use panels of bleached and stamped artwork. Thin, undiluted household bleach was used to stamp with. Experiment with different types of card stock and always remember to clean your stamps immediately after use. Heating the stamped image will intensify the bleaching effect and will also dry the card before further stamping and embossing is done. Both cards were further embellished with threaded beads.

Embellishments

An embellishment, to me, is anything that adds to the finish of a design. Embellishments can vary from craft stickers, crystals, buttons, beads and brads to ribbons and pressed flowers. The list is seemingly endless and the possibilities infinite. Use your imagination and experiment, but avoid overzealous embellishment as this can detract from, rather than enhance, the finished design. Remember: less is more.

The subtly stamped design above was embellished with tiny punched tags, coordinating threads and pre-printed vellum. The colour theme was repeated in the backing panels and matte-finish brads.
A stamped and embossed panel was used as the centre piece for the design at the top of the page. It was then embellished using triangular pieces of card and wrapped thread in coordinating colours.

Butterfly Dance

This project features some of the more traditional embellishments, namely craft stickers and crystals, as well as the less conventional dimensional glaze. It also features a more complicated masking technique than was used in the chalked flower project (pages 60–64).

The frame surrounding the two butterflies slightly overlaps the tips of their wings. This creates the impression that they are being viewed through a window, adding a feeling of depth to the finished design.

You will need

- Rubber stamps (Letter Background 1999L by Penny Black and Embroidered Butterfly E6079 by Impression Obsession)
- Pad of repositionable notes
- A4 sheet of cream card
- Pearlescent paper – two purple pieces 7.5 x 15cm (3 x 6in), two turquoise pieces 7.5 x 12cm (3 x 4¾in) and two dark blue pieces 7.5 x 9.5cm (3 x 3¾in)
- Cream card blank, 18 x 13cm (7 x 5in)
- Spare paper
- Self-healing cutting mat
- Multicoloured dye-based inkpad
- Black dye-based inkpad
- Clear embossing powder
- Teaspoon
- Heat gun
- Old CD
- Waterbrush or small paintbrush
- Guillotine or scissors
- Craft knife
- Double-sided sticky tape
- Tiny crystals
- PVA glue in a fine-tipped applicator bottle
- Stick of uncooked spaghetti
- Dimensional glaze
- Gold border craft stickers and gold square craft stickers

1. Work on a cutting mat with a sheet of spare paper laid over the top. Ink the butterfly stamp using the black dye-based inkpad.

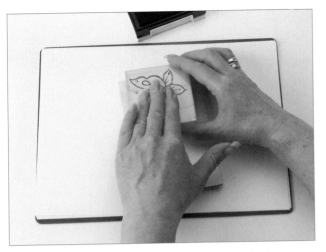

2. Stamp the butterfly image on to the pad of repositionable notes (make sure it overlays the sticky part of the paper).

3. Tear off two sheets together.

4. Cut out the design, making sure you cut on the lines and not outside them. There is no need to cut out the antennae.

5. Peel the two butterflies apart – you will use these as masks when you start to create your design.

6. Stamp a butterfly image on to the A4 sheet of cream card using the black dye-based inkpad. Cover with clear embossing powder, tap off the excess and heat. Stamp a second image on to the card.

7. Cover the second image with clear embossing powder.

8. Tap off the excess powder.

9. Heat the image until the embossing powder has melted.

10. Attach the masks you made earlier to the two butterfly images.

11. Ink up the background stamp using the multicoloured dye-based inkpad.

12. Stamp the background image on to the card, covering one of the butterfly images. Make sure you press firmly all over the stamp.

13. Carefully lift off the stamp.

14. Stamp the background over the second butterfly image. Be careful that the two background images do not overlap. Peel off the two masks.

15. Transfer ink from the inkpad to an old CD to create a palette.

16. Pick up the ink by pressing the CD firmly on to the inkpad.

17. Using a waterbrush or a small paintbrush, colour the butterflies.

18. Use one colour at a time. Cleaning each colour off the brush before using the next one by wiping it on a spare piece of paper.

19. Trim the edges of the design using a guillotine or a pair of scissors to create a rectangular panel.

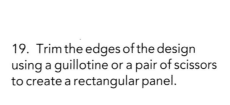

20. Place the two purple pearlescent paper strips back to back and cut them on the diagonal to create four triangles. Do the same with the turquoise and dark blue paper pieces.

21. Attach double-sided sticky tape to the back of the butterfly panel. Stick a dark blue triangle to the top right-hand corner leaving a narrow blue border.

22. Attach another dark blue triangle to the bottom left-hand corner, again leaving a narrow blue border.

23. Turn the design over and attach double-sided sticky tape as before.

24. Attach a purple triangle to the top left-hand corner, and one to the bottom right, again creating a narrow border around the corners of the design.

Tip

Peel back the top layer of each strip of tape to half way along its length, then remove it completely once the triangle is in place.

25. To complete the design, attach turquoise triangles to the top right-hand and bottom left-hand corners using the same technique as above.

26. Attach the butterfly design to the front of the card blank using double-sided sticky tape.

27. Apply narrow gold border craft stickers around the edges of the design.

28. To obtain a neat finish, tuck the ends of the stickers under the paper background.

29. Attach three square, gold-coloured craft stickers to the bottom right-hand corner of the card. Attach three smaller ones to the top left-hand corner of the design. Use a craft knife to manipulate them into position.

30. Put a spot of PVA glue where each tiny crystal will be positioned – on the ends of the antennae, on the tips of the wings and on each of the square, gold craft stickers.

31. Pick up each crystal using the dampened end of the stick of spaghetti and position it on the card.

32. Finally, add dimensional glaze to the patterns on the upper wings and leave it to dry overnight. This gives the image a three-dimensional appearance.

The completed project.

The stamped and coloured panel on the top card had its corners punched using a south-west corner punch. This is a quick method of embellishing a panel. It can be made more decorative by adding metallic thread. Some elegant scrolled craft stickers were added to this design to further highlight the corners.

This textured card shown bottom right has stamped and sponged panels and was simply embellished with three small crystals. Crystals were also placed at the centre of each flower. Mounting a stamped image on to black glossy card and trimming to leave a narrow border is the simplest of all embellishments, but leads to a truly professional finish. This is illustrated by the bottom left-hand card in the picture above.

The top left-hand card was created by weaving stamped paper strips into a background panel. This was then decorated with punched vellum daisies embellished with black and white daisy craft stickers.

The geometric black and white card shown top right uses stamped and embossed images, 3D adhesive foam squares and crystals to embellish two basic square panels.

A small floral diamond stamp was stamped and embossed in both black and white to create the bottom right-hand card. The panel on which the shapes were mounted was further embellished using a floral corner punch. Thin, undiluted household bleach was used to paint the flowers, and as a finishing touch some crystals were added.

The bottom left-hand card once again used woven paper strips to create the main focus. A hint of colour was added with the addition of two stamped and embossed flowers. The flower was completed with a crystal centre and wire stem.

Index

Nine small floral panels were further embellished with tiny crystals and black square craft stickers in this simple yet highly effective card.